DISCOVER SERIES
TOOLS

INSTRUMENTOS

Allen Wrench

Llave Allen

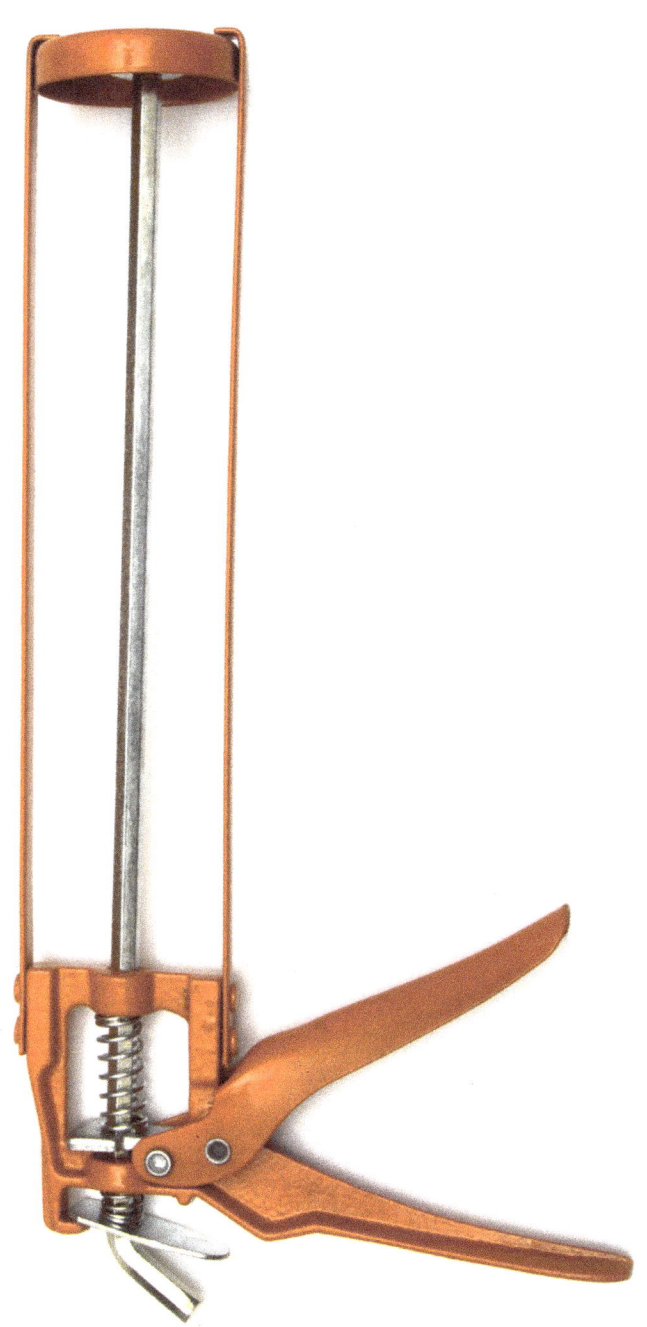

Pistola de Calafateo

Caulking Gun

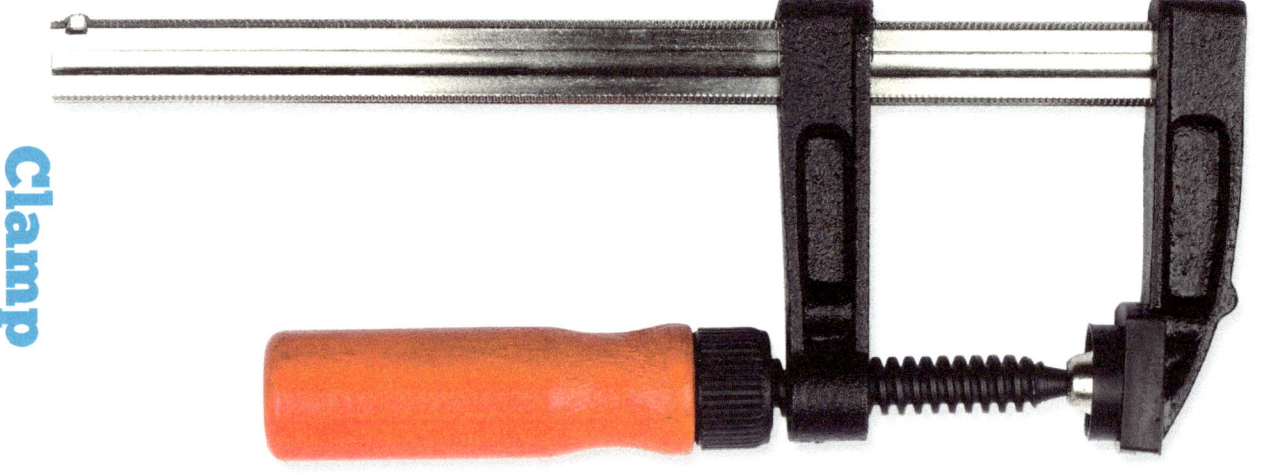

Clamp — **Abrazadera**

Finishing Hammer

Martillo de acabado

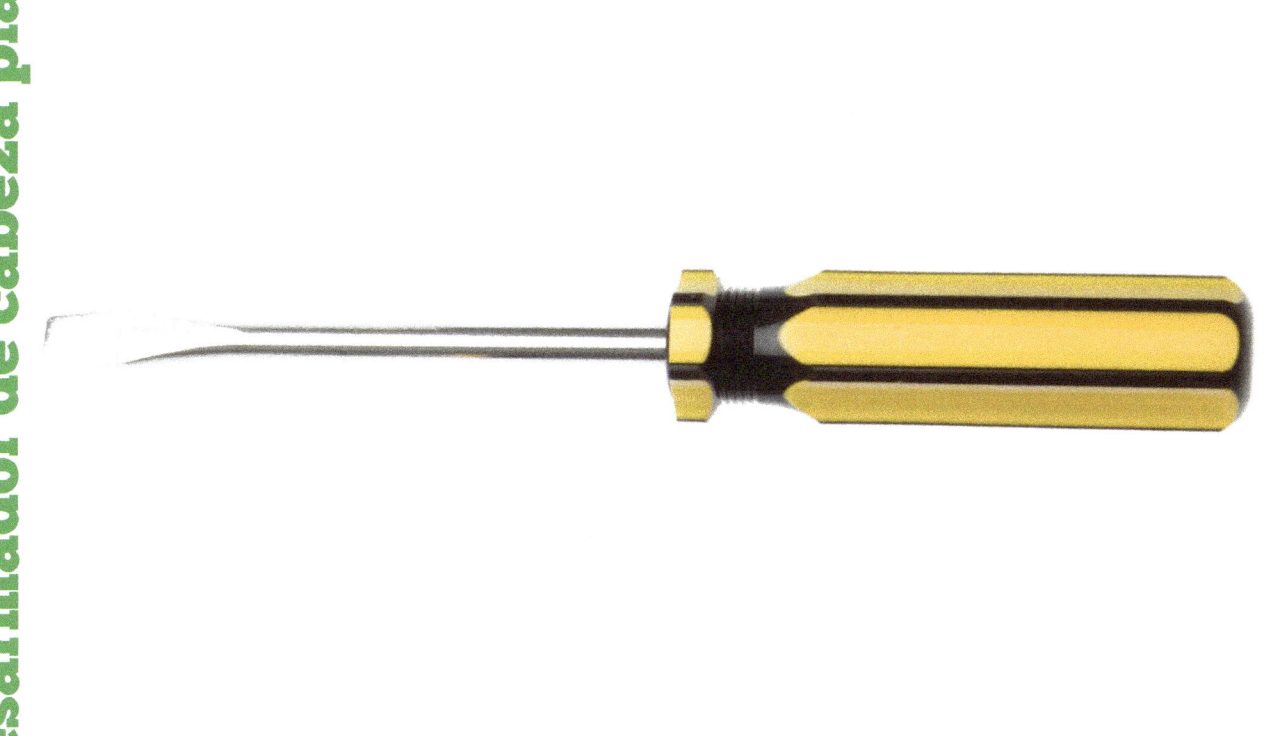

Desarmador de cabeza plana

Flat Head Screwdriver

Framing Hammer — Martillo para marco

Guantes  **Gloves**

Casco **Hard Hat**

Hatchet / **Hacha**

Mazo — Mallet

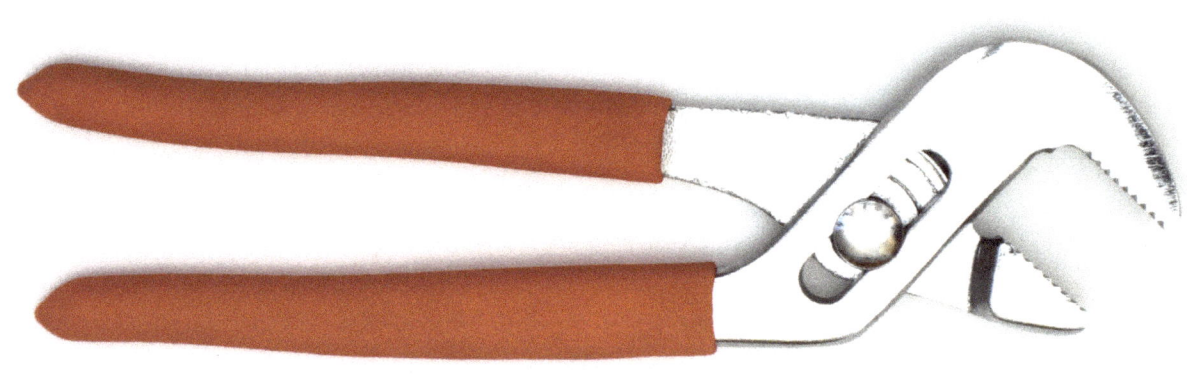

Monkey Wrench

Llave inglesa

Clavos 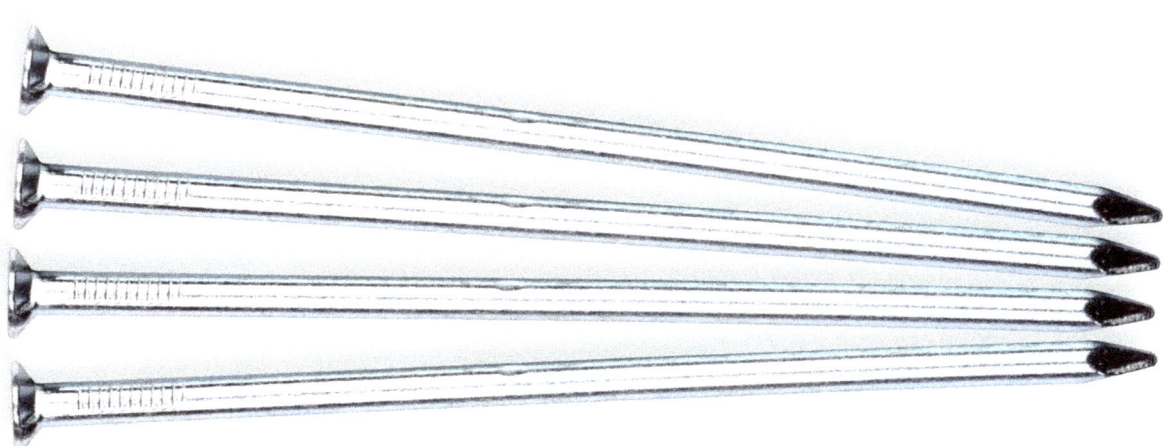 **Nails**

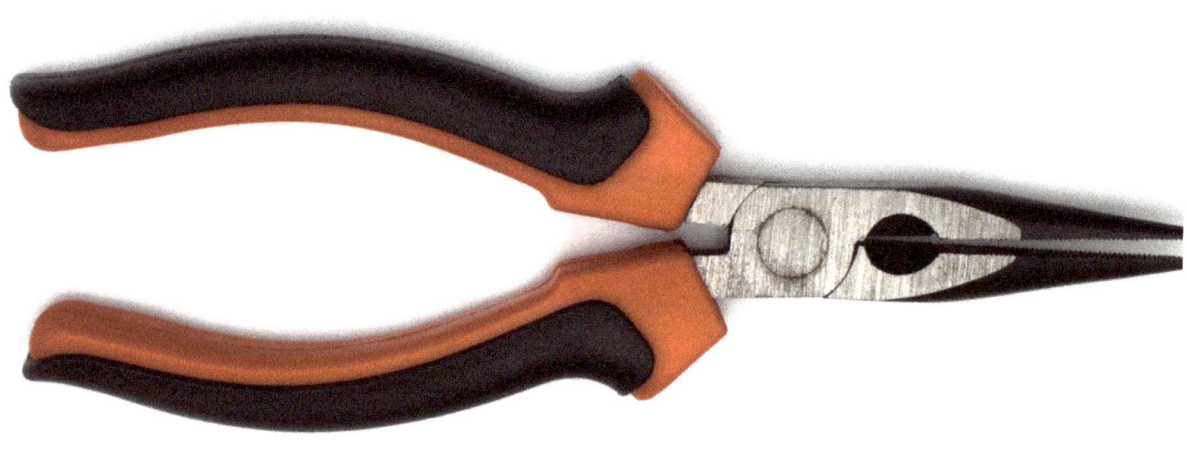

Needle Nose Pliers

Pinzas de punta de aguja

Brocha   **Paint Brush**

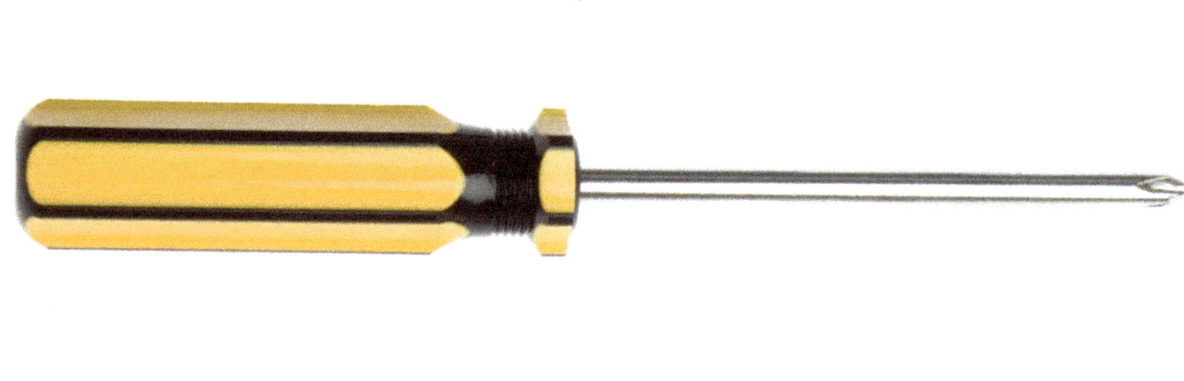

Phillips Screwdriver

Desarmador de cruz

Pinzas 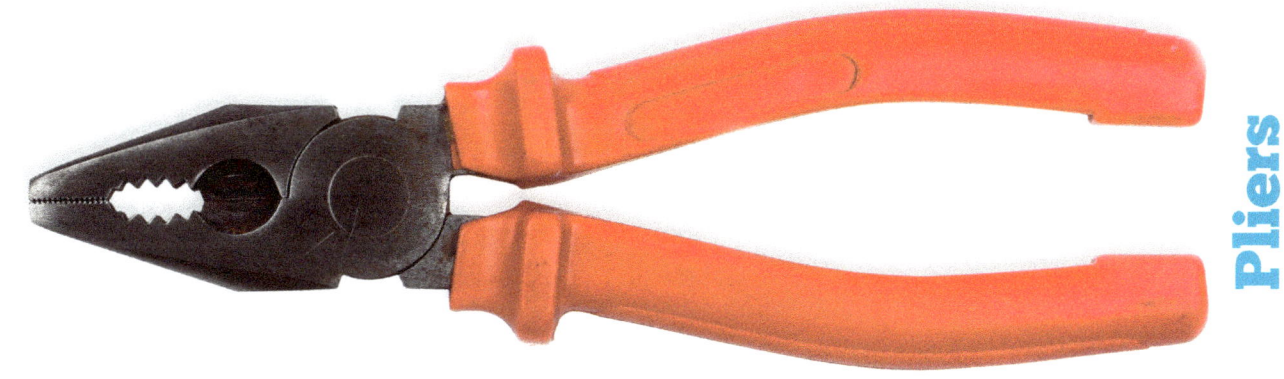 **Pliers**

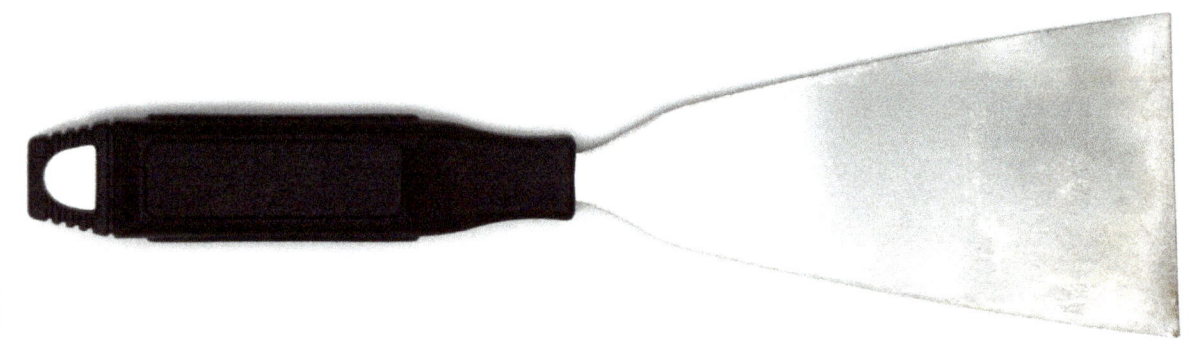

Putty Knife

Cuchillo para macilla

Navaja

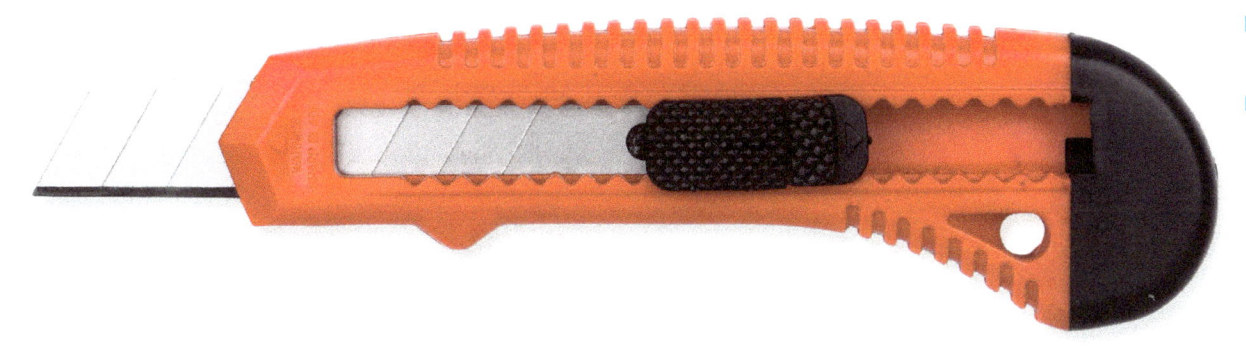

Razor Blade

Ruler   Regla

Tornillos

Screws

Pistola de grapas

Staple Gun

Cinta Metrica

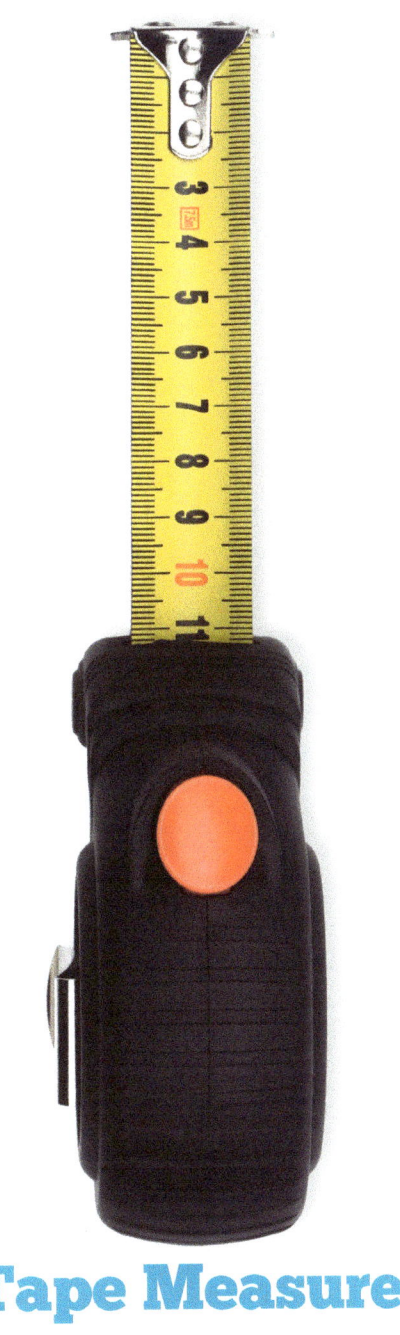

Tape Measure

Nivelador

Torpedo Level

Desforradora de Alambres

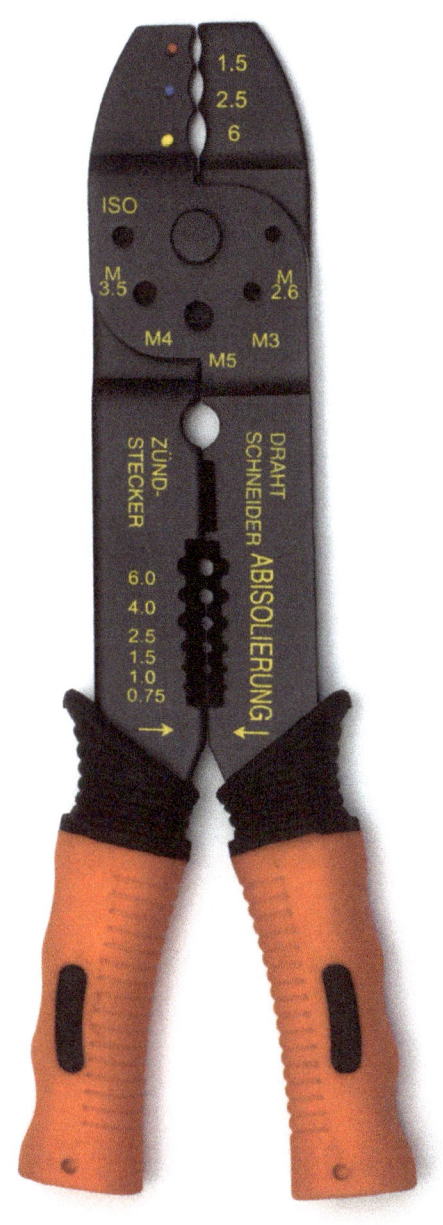

Wire Strippers

Llave inglesa

Wrench

Make Sure to Check Out the Other Discover Series Books from Xist Publishing:

Published in the United States by Xist Publishing
www.xistpublishing.com
PO Box 61593 Irvine, CA 92602

© 2018 by Xist Publishing All rights reserved
Translated by Lenny Sandoval
No portion of this book may be reproduced without express permission of the publisher
All images licensed from Fotolia
First Bilingual Edition

ISBN: 978-1-5324-0774-1   eISBN: 978-1-5324-0775-8

xist Publishing